10 commandments of game design

Welcome.

I've made every type of game under the sun. This book is the culmination of twenty years of professional game development, but moreover, a lifetime of being a sponge to not only game development and design, but the creative process and the processes of others.

This book is intentionally concise.

Ignore these commandments at your own peril.

They must be followed to reach success.

ISBN: 1977898580
ISBN-13: 978-1977898586

DEDICATION

My family.

ACKNOWLEDGMENTS

I would like to thank the amazing teams that I have been a part of over years, from my family to Konami, to Forge Father, the dedicated developers are what gets me out of bed each morning.

Thank you,

J.R.

COMMANDMENTS

COMMANDMENT 0:

TOOLS OF THE TRADE

This book assumes a few things:

- You have an internet connection and a computer.
- You can read, have eyes, hands and ears.

NOTE:

- If at any time you find yourself saying *'but I don't have x'* - Stop, and go get x.
  - If you are a student - talk to your professors or classmates.
- If you are a professional, ask yourself how you got to where you are and where you want to be.

It's time to put your big kid pants on.

'That which impedes your task, is your task.'

-Unknown

Using the right tools is critical to Game Development.

I use:

PHOTOSHOP ($20/month sub. fee)

- This is vital for prototyping (Commandment 5) and iteration (Commandment 6).
- There are free alternatives. Find them.

3DS MAX (Free Student Version)

- You must have some sort of modeling program to create basic primitives in the game engine.

GAME ENGINE (Unreal, Free)

- Unreal is a beast and it has amazing video documentation and tutorials. I have used it for most of my game projects and it is amazing.

SLACK (Free)

- Communication with your team is absolutely critical. Your team may consist of hundreds of developers or just you and your cat/muse/subconscience.

GOOGLE DRIVE (Free)

- **<u>WRITE. SHIT. DOWN.</u>**
- See Documentation, Commandment 9.

PERFORCE (Free)

- This one is an industry secret. It keeps all of the files backed up so that you never lose anything.
- **This is absolutely critical** and will transform your project from *amateur hour* to pro status.
- Use a cloud storage service like Digital Ocean ($20/mo.) to host your perforce (p4).
- Without P4 setup, don't bother. Seriously.

TEAM (Free)

- Surround yourself with like-minded individuals that are motivated and see the goal.
- Create a Hook and Vision (Commandment 3) that everyone can get behind. Refer back to it often to keep the project on track.
- Team members will come and go, and personalities will often dominate different aspects of the project - but it is the team that is the single most important tool of the development process and you must learn to work together towards the common goal.

These are the critical tools of the trade. This only covers game development - and not business development - that is an entirely other book. Design and development is a small piece of the success puzzle. Let's continue.

COMMANDMENT 1: MAKE IT FUN

Nobody ever plays shitty games. Nobody ever says *'Hey man, have you played X? It's terrible and I spend ten hours a day on it.'*

Nope. Not happening. Your game must be fun.

There are a number of other books about finding fun, and what fun is exactly and it is different for everyone. There have been academic papers with big data quantifying what most players like, or what sells best and common threads. If there was a single answer - everyone would use it, plain and simple.

There are a number of mobile games that use tight loops (Game Loop, Commandment 8) - this is merely a simple method of rewarding the player for accomplishing a task.

- Players seek reward and power.

Both reward and power operate on the subconscious mind and are incredibly addicting. There is a great Tedx talk about Dopamine and Porn Addiction - view it now.

Summed up, it is the designers job to get the consumer addicted to their product.

It's pretty fucked up - but developers and publishers are not out for the betterment of the individual - but instead they are running a business that needs consumers to purchase, and continue to purchase their product in order for the business to be successful.

Making it fun boils down to a few key items:

- Start with a unique Hook (Commandment 3)
- Iteration on that Hook (Chapter 6)

Hook and Vision which we cover in detail in Commandment 3 is the big idea. Big ideas are pretty worthless until you:

- Write it down.
- Act on it.

Writing down your idea will help you shape it into a pitch and help you begin to figure out what it is you are making and the scope of it.

We have all heard people say *'I had that idea'* or *'I invented that'* or something similar. If these idiots wrote it down then acted on it, they would be the ones celebrating a product launch and not watching someone else do it. The ones celebrating are the ones who wrote it down and acted on it. You must do the same.

Writing it down also gives you and your project the basis for copyright and/or patent, which is all any investor will ask for when you try to raise capital. (Book II - Business)

Writing it down will help you define exactly what your game is - and allow you to tell others about it - and get feedback. This is part of the feedback and iteration loop. It will also immediately help you figure out if people, friends, family think it is fun, or even understandable.

Many call this the 'mom test' or 'wife test'. This simply refers to finding people outside your immediate circle who may not have any idea what it is you are talking about - so making it understandable and fun for them is a good indicator for a broader audience. When I was developing Thon, I would test with my designer friends, gamer friends, mom groups, family and kids. You will also want focus groups and testers once you have a concise and playable version.

This leads us to *act on it*. All this means is once you have started to write down what it is your are making, you will begin to find gaping holes in your designs or concepts that will emerge that will sound cool or complement the design. Write all of this down as well - make notes. I use regular old yellow sticky notes and re-type them into Google Drive when I am done. I keep a pocket notebook (moleskine) with me at all times and label the projects on the spine. I go through two-three of these notebooks every month. Many ideas are pushed to later or iterated on until they morph into something else entirely. Keeping good notes, writing it down, then prototyping (Commandment 5) and Iterating (Commandment 6) is absolutely vital.

Your development loop should look something like this:

- Initial Idea - written down
- Test idea
- Take notes
- Revise Idea based on notes
- Test some more
- Continue this loop until all notes/testing is complete.
- Move on to next idea.

There are two very broad targets for your game;

- Make what you like = small niche audience.
- Make what the market likes = broader audience.

Defining what the market wants is tough. It is safer, cheaper and easier to make something small and simple and target a niche market, carve out a space for yourself, then expand.

Balance or the appearance of balance will turn players on or off. If a player feels powerful, they will play your game and think it is fun. If it feels imbalanced they will feel weak and leave. Getting a player to feel is what good design is all about - it is many layers of feedback, effects, touch, lights, cameras, action, and epic moments. It is the designers job to first concept this, then explain it to the team in the Vision, then bring the team together to craft the experience. This has always been referred to as design, but the newish buzzword is UX - User Experience.

The same is true for movies - but games have one enormous advantage - the double-edged sword of interactivity. We hand off to the user and allow them to craft, or completely fuck up their experience. A tight design can improve the experience but no design is flawless. We just do our best and learn from mistakes.

Power is a good motivator - as is progress. If players feel that they aren't getting anywhere, they will shelve your game. There are a number of methods to display progress; the aptly named progress bar, experience bar, a map, fog of war, a road, level meter, numbers, stats, you name it. Anything that can be built on, improved and progressed teaches the player they are getting somewhere and their time has been well spent.

Customization is another good motivator for fun, progress and power. Look at the success of something like World of Warcraft - massive amounts of customization - each character is different - it allows players to create their ideal selves and escape into a realm where anything is possible.

Customization is not limited to billion-dollar games. It can be something as simple as changing the fonts or colors of your user-interface. Any amount of customization allows personalization and ownership. Players get vested and are less likely to shelve the game if they are invested in it.

Fun can also be defined simply as an improvement over what is already available. Can your game improve on;

- Story
- Existing
- Price

Can your game be the same as something else but have a better story? Invest in a writer or back-engineer the target story and make yours better. Make flow charts of story branches and explore all options. Maybe your version is better, maybe it isn't. What if Vader wasn't Luke's father?

Is there something already out there or have you made something already that you can improve on? Once you have made your first title - improve on it and release something new and better. Clash of Clans released Clash Royale and killed it. ARMA spawned DayZ, then H1, and now PUBG - and at the time of writing - PUBG just surpassed 1.5 million concurrent on steam. PUBG never would have existed if someone hadn't first made ARMA, then DAYZ.

Price. Can you undercut the competition? Welcome to capitalism. As soon as you complete your project, and have any amount of success, someone will do the same thing for less. You will have to do it better (refer to Story/Existing) or do it for less.

Let's continue.

COMMANDMENT 2:
20 DEVS / 2 YEARS

The team is vital and the scope will determine the size of the team and the timeframe. There is a book about rapid development that breaks down the product development process into a triangle of; Workers, Time, Money.

That's it. That's all you get.

'Workers' is generally the flexible X-factor and why so many game companies crunch their employees to death or lawsuit. The ship date is generally unmovable - we must make Christmas. The budget is generally unwavering - we must fit within the investor's budget. If either of these move then the project will overspend and not make back the money that was spent, and the company will fold.

Workers are expendable. When you are the one running the company, it is the harsh reality. If your employees don't like it, they can leave and you can find a replacement. That said, some employees are hard to replace - high level senior developers or those that pull more than their share should be kept on.

Lately, there has been a shift with some of the most successful companies treating their employees far better, providing food, nap rooms, additional vacation, etc. Crunching employees over eighty-hour weeks just leads to burnout and them eventually hating the company and leaving only to do it again somewhere else.

When you are first starting out, you will be working on your game after hours - you need to make time to create your product. Find the hours. Side projects are built from 8pm to 1am 7 days a week. There is no vacation time when you are first developing your project and you will love it - once you drop into the right frame of mind and decide what your goal is and how to accomplish it.

Non-developers and friends will fall by the wayside and that is ok. You will begin to change your peer group to those that are like-minded and motivated. The better your circle of peers, the better the product.

- You are the five people you associate with most. Make it count.

20 Devs.

You can certainly make a game with fewer or with more - but 20 is roughly the number of people you will want to finish a AA game in about 2 years. Yours may vary, and often when first starting, devs will wear many hats - I find generally there are:

- Artistic Designer
- Coder Designer

The Artistic Designer has some art background, can model, mockup, animate, paint or generally create an interesting look and feel. Their background may be in Art and they have good ideas, or at least *big* ideas and they throw them into the pot and get cooking. They are creatives and dreamers. I fall into this category.

The Coder Designer is adept at coding, visual studio, scripting and general logic. They are typically more of a critical thinker. They are the yin-yang and balance to the dreamer. They help ground the Artistic Designers dream-balloon before it floats too far off into space.

They are often the ones asking and answering the critical question: HOW THE FUCK ARE WE GOING TO DO THAT?

The team then collaborates and comes up with solution and prototypes. Then repeat.

There are many roles and the larger the team the more specialized each role becomes. I have worked on massive projects with hundreds of devs as well as tiny 1-2 man teams. Both have strengths and weaknesses.

In a large team you generally have these disciplines:

- Art
- Code
- Design
- Business

Art

These are animators, 3d artists, concept artists, fx artists and tech artists. There are all different titles and definitions and each company is different, but these are generally the main ones and the ones you will want to fill in order to have a well-oiled team.

Code

Programmers. With the release of high-level free engines the role of the coder has slightly changed. If you are writing your own game engine, you will want one. Otherwise - think critically about whether you need to change engine content or can simply build it in a blueprint.

Design

Designers must be problem solvers. They have to fix what is broken or dream up some solution - some interesting gameplay - to fix the boring status quo of the market - There are narrative/writers, level/area designers, systems designers, mechanics, and scripters. The designers are the ideas guys - but they then must prototype that idea and show it to the team and get everyone on board. Design is an evolving and iterative process. The team MUST understand this.

- The game isn't done until it is on the shelf.

After a year or more of development, after the level has been handed off to art to complete - there will be a second pass at updating the game with the more interesting gameplay components and removing those that are not working, broken or won't have time to improve. Often this will make or break a team. Artists will complain that their work was done - but it isn't. There is still time for improvement. This leads us to the industry's 'C' word. Crunch.

Crunch simply put, is long hours and long weeks. Devs will put in 60-80 or more hours in a week. Do the math - that is all weekend, and all week. You barely have time to shower, eat and do laundry.

Crunch typically occurs at the end of the project, but some studios will have mini-crunches every month or bi-weekly milestone, where they attempt to get back lost time or stay on top of the project before it spirals too far off course.

A project director, producer or director will have a close eye on progress and the ship date. If progress isn't meeting the target - devs will have to crunch or content will be cut. It is almost always devs crunching. There are a number of reasons - scope is too big, bugs causing major issues, software problems, etc, but the main reason for crunch is terrible or non-existent individual time management - the devs just aren't working.

'In hell, it's always 2-4pm'

A typical entry-level or mid-level developer's day at a AAA studio looks like this:

930a	Wake up and drag ass out of bed
10a	Arrive at office
10-10:30a	Coffee, socialize
10:30-11a	Check email, schedule, social media, talk shop
11:30a	Scrum/Meeting or start work from last night
11:45a	Begin lunch plans
Noon	Leave office for lunch
1:30	Return from lunch
1:20-2	Food coma, socialize, social media
2-4	Work
4	Break. Coffee, walk. Bitch about the company.
330-630	Work
630-7	Wrap that shit up. Socialize. Criticize the guy that leaves at 6.
7	Leave office, eat fast food, commute.

Add in your 8-midnight or later gaming sessions and you have a recipe for disaster. Repeat.

- Controlling your time is the single most important aspect of health and wealth.

Have you ever called a doctor and told them the time for your appointment? No. The Dr. tells you what time your appointment is. It is society's pecking order. The Dr. controls their time and is fulfilled on a deeper level.

My schedule;

430	Leap out of bed.
	Coffee/breakfast
	Identify critical issues and goals for the day
	Creative Zone
630	Feed my kids, pack bags review their day
8	Drop them at school
8–9	Workout
9-1130	Work. Goals are set and accomplished
1130	Lunch
12-2	Work
2-6	Work tedium. This is where I knock out bugs, and general annoyances
	Low cognitive area
6-8	Dinner and family time, walk
8-10	Work wrap up
	Identify what worked and didn't for the next day.

I have this schedule 7 days/week.
Repeat

Senior-level devs will have better time management - they are responsible for their area, the area of another dev, or a will have several team members assigned to them - so they must have their shit together.

- Crunch is just a studio's way of getting back the time the devs have pissed away.

When you are running a team, you will need to manage the other devs. Start with your immediate circle and ramp up. Begin working with old and current co-workers or other students.

You will need to develop a budget and timeframe for the projects. You will need to hire or get devs that can get the job done and scale accordingly. If your game can only be done for $5 billion, you will need to adjust. Start small and have a clear Vision. Write down every feature, prop and asset in a spreadsheet and assign a time and cost to it. This will give you your timeframe and budget. Continually add or remove new assets or obsolete one. The spreadsheet is a living document and the heart of the project. A good financial projection will be the only thing an investor asks for when you first pitch your concept. This is critical - it lets the investor know you have thought through the entire project and you actually know what it will cost and how long it will take. Then they will ask you to do it faster and for less. Let's continue.

COMMANDMENT 3:

HOOK AND VISION

The game hook and vision are critical. They are the elevator pitch that will get people listening or investing. If your game sounds flat, no one will play it. You must have a concise hook and vision.

- A good hook is the game's gimmick:
  - What do you do?
  - What is it about?

The hook is a critical component and what your documentation (Commandment 9) will detail. If you can't sum it up in an interesting one-liner, it's not that interesting and nobody will pay attention.

Read some IMDB movie tag lines to get a good feel for what makes a good pitch or hook. The design documentation will detail what the world is about if someone is interested.

It is here that you and your team will need to answer the following questions:

- Why would anyone play this?
- What are we making?
- What is already available?
- How do we improve?

The answers may come easy, they most likely will not. You will have to prototype (Commandment 5) and iterate (Commandment 6) to find the answers - but you need to have it written down to set the vision to guide the development.

On Fallout, the answer was pretty simple: More. Fallout is already an established powerhouse and people want more of it. So we added hundreds of quests, amazing companions and cool items and features. It was more of everything people already liked and wanted. It was a slam dunk.

When establishing a new IP, or breathing new life into an old one, you have to be extra critical. On Tomb Raider Legend, Crystal Dynamics was given the opportunity to revitalize Lara. We were ecstatic - one of the largest IP's in games in our hands. The direction was pretty clear - the last few TR games have had abysmal reviews and waning interest - and Lara handled like a tank. We focused entirely on puzzles and fluid movement. We got Toby Gard on board and he brought with him a demo of a sort of free-climbing movement system he had been working on. It was awesome and everyone was excited - Toby pitched the team on the movement - and we wanted the movement. Legend's fluid movement was born, and TR was reborn.

*NOTE: I'll never forget an old classmate, upon hearing of Crystals opportunity, ask me what my plans were for 'Tom.' Puzzled, I inquired. He said with a smirk: 'Tom. Tom Braider.'

As goofy as it was, it also helped me put things in perspective. The vast majority of people don't give a shit about our games. We have to love developing it otherwise it is meaningless. You have to have passion. You have to love what you do. You have to have Vision.

COMMANDMENT 4: AI

Do you remember the movie A.I.? I never saw it. I took word of mouth reviews for face value and didn't go. Moral of the story - you must decide where you are going to spend your time. At the movies or developing your game. Are you deciding who is making it, and what goes in the game, who you fight and why? Or is someone else?

If your game is using AI you must put some development time into it. If your game is Multiplayer/player versus player - you will need to look into servers, hosting, joining, etc. which is outside the scope of this book. Also assume you only have a life cycle of one year, at best - before people stop playing your game. Dead servers, dead game.

Artificial Intelligence - AI, are generally the game's antagonists. A newish term is PVE - Player Versus Environment.

You will have a designer, or programmer, or you, designing enemies and their behaviors. They will need a unique silhouette, range, mobility, amount, and many other factors. I made a simple acronym called R-MASK to design enemies, it breaks down like so;

R	Range
M	Mobility
A	Amount
S	Survivability
K	Killing Power

Range: Pretty self-explanatory, but, this is their attack range. Are they close combat only, mid-level, or a sniper? Do they toggle modes? Transform?

Mobility: Speed. How fast is this guy? Immobile turret? Fast zombie? Teleport. Think of game-relevant movement.

Amount: Quantity that spawns in. Spawning in 100 tanks when you only have a pistol is shit. 1 tank, some weaker fodder guys and a couple of mid-level guys is a better setup. Most game engines can't handle too many enemies. This is why they come in waves. Be mindful of quantities when developing and designing setups.

Survivability: Health, hit points, armor, durability. Fodder guys have low HP, tanks have high HP. The silhouette should probably match - but mixing size and strength can lead to some cool enemy types. Also, don't forget coloration - the red ones are always tougher.

Killing Power: This is how hard it hits. Again, zombie close combat fodder, swarmer, probably shouldn't one-hit you, but that tank round should. Unless you are also a tank or capital ship or planet-eating planet. (Unicron!)

Combining these into interesting AI is only part of it - the other part, and a huge part of iterative gameplay design is a good combat setup. A good setup has a flow to it - peaks and valleys. It engages the player's subconscious, *'Am I going to die?'* and triggers dopamine to get them addicted once they survive and get their reward, be it resources to play more or phat loots (tm ;)

The AI and level design should work closely together - often teams will build entire gameplay areas - only to have a mechanic change mid-development that will render the area obsolete, or require major rework. This is where the majority of a level designers time will be spent - iterating on the layout and combat setups. If you have a large team with specialized designers - they will need to work side-by-side to identify issues, solutions and improvements.

If you have a smaller team, this will either be entirely on your shoulders, or the shoulders of one or two devs - possibly working remotely - and will need to communicate via images, video, skype, or Slack. It works fine and more devs are moving to remote positions - I highly recommend it.

NOTE: Remote staff also vastly increases your quality level of the team as you are able to recruit internationally rather than just locally, or with people willing to relocate. (I should have covered this in team.)

AI should provide some level of challenge. Depending on your design vision, target demographic and overall goal the AI will vary greatly. Take for example something like Dark Souls - very difficult vs. Candy Crush, simple.
Balancing AI is difficult and time consuming. It requires tuning when the game isn't complete - so testers - probably you and the team - will be combating enemies with only partially completed game mechanics for the majority of development. It is vital that you prototype (Chapter 5) and Iterate (Chapter 6) constantly and keep

both the AI and the player's mechanics balanced. If the game is not a challenge, player's will breeze through it and get bored and shelve it. If the game is too difficult, player's will feel powerless, and shelve it. This is often why games have difficulty settings and a primary motivator for multiplayer cheaters - they want the power but not the discipline or commitment to earn it.

Let's continue.

COMMANDMENT 5: PROTOTYPE

There are a number of great prototyping tools available;
- blank playing cards (Amazon)
- Game Engines
- Sketches (notebook, Photoshop)
- Write it down (Google Drive, Cards)

EXAMPLE:

- Use a template in Unreal, block out basic gameplay.
- Jump around, run around, shoot.
- Move blocks and gameplay items until it works and there is no confusion on the direction.
- Go upstairs and ask your mom to come down and play it. (heyoo)
- Work on the basics - the character or main mechanic that you have established in your Vision and Hook.
- This will take a lot of iteration. (Chapter 6)
- We know what we are fighting against, from Chapter 4 - AI, so make some iterations on one or two AI.
- Build the mechanic or fake it, and mock it up in edited game footage.

WILL IT WORK?

Pitching a game demo to an investor is easier if you have a Minimum Viable Product - MVP - or simply, a playable version of your game. It proves to the investor you are serious, you have invested money and sweat 'sweat equity' and can get it done.

- You can skip directly to this stage and pitch this. straight away by demonstrating mechanics.
- Build a Game demo.
- Mechanics should focus on something new, your hook or gimmick;
- What is your gimmick? - in actual use.
- Requires a lot of changes.
- Requires a lot of testing.
- You should probably have dedicated QA of some kind.
- Wife/gf/Mom test.

HARDWARE

Hardware is the single largest bottleneck in game development. We are developing products on dated hardware as soon as we start. Even when a company receives next-gen specs, we must fit the big idea into a tiny box. Hardware is the single biggest limiter - if you want to make some real money - bypass the hardware and find distribution. Some companies have tried cloud-engines but there is currently nothing readily available or working well. Microsoft, Sony and Valve are on top because they have platforms that are widely distributed.

Hardware is a limiter because the game must fit within the hardware spec, memory and size limits. I spent more time downloading Destiny than playing it - and I thought it was an amazing game. The point is, games can be huge, and require downloads, patching or multiple discs.

- You must think about distribution when designing your game.

 If you plan to use consoles, you must get through their process which can be lengthy at best. You must fill out applications, read documentation and eventually submit, probably multiple times for approval. From their perspective, it acts as a filter to prevent too much garbage from reaching the market. Let's continue.

COMMANDMENT 6: ITERATION

What is iteration?

Iteration means:
- Play the game.
- Listen to the voice in your head or of others.
- Write it down!
- Play the game.

In Commandment 5, we talked about the prototype - actually making the hook. Without iteration - you will never discover the best parts of your game.

Iteration means focusing on a single gameplay aspect and testing it constantly until it works as designed, or it is improved beyond the initial design. This can take hours or months or even years.

- Focus on hourly iteration.
- Iteration = Innovation

During development, the designer will prototype a mechanic, or mock something up, or 'hack something'. The team will test the mechanic and provide feedback. If the team likes the direction or comes up with a new one, devs will be assigned to finishing it or making variations broken up over the project's schedule. As each new iteration comes together, the team will meet, discuss and further iterate. The schedule must be updated to reflect this or you risk missing your ship date. Things must stay fluid and move around, get extra hours, or be cut.

Example - Jump Mechanic

'That jump should be higher, or longer.' Or *'that animation should be faster, or slower.'*

Some changes are quick and easy to implement, others are not and will take time.

- Balance iteration with time and budget.

On Dungeon Siege, I was assigned to developing the camera and dialogue systems for the NPC conversations. The problem was, the programmer assigned to them wasn't working on them yet - so there was a very limited tool available. I started with documentation (Commandment 9) and wrote it like a flow chart. I handed it off to QA and asked them to walk through the document step by step to see if they could implement in-game content based on the steps. If they were not, I reviewed where it broke down, then iterated on the document and reevaluated it. Documentation will need to be iterated on and mechanics developed in the proper order. Your game is like a snake; the head must know where it is going and the body must fall in line. When you are setting up your spreadsheet, make sure each disciplines timeframe lines up with whichever other disciplines are dependant on them. You can't have animators animating models that haven't been concepted or built yet.*

(Mostly true, Unreal can use the same skeletons across multiple models, provided they are rigged correctly.)

There will be a point during development where the game turns the corner from being a clusterfuck of mechanics that don't work and are smashed together, to a functioning game. This is always an exciting time as you begin to see the actual fun that was designed and implemented and everyone's hard work begins to pay off. This has a snowball effect and can really motivate a team to finish off the product.

- Most developers do not play the games they make.

Of all of the studios I've worked at, and all of the games I have shipped, only a tiny fraction of devs actually play the game and provide feedback to the team. There are a number of reasons for this.

- Game budgets and timelines are extremely tight, so there isn't time for devs to be doing anything other than their assigned tasks.
  - If a dev misses their deadline, the entire project is affected. If a dev doesn't play the game, nobody will notice.
- The majority of the team has no fucking clue what they are making, because;
- Documentation is non-existent, terrible or too long.
- ...and because of that, the majority of the feedback is useless or will require assets that are not available or within budget.
  - We will rectify this in COMMANDMENT 9.
- It is up to the individual dev to understand the scope of the game, and in general, they don't care,

because most devs don't get to work on the types of games they like - they are there for a paycheck.

- The majority of studios do not ever communicate the schedule or budget or make it available.

- There are two types of team management: Glass and Black Box and you will need to decide which you are going to be and why. Both have extreme benefits and liabilities. Details of these styles is outside the scope of this book, but basically you tell the team everything, or you tell them on a need-to-know basis.
  - Tell them everything and they feel engaged, but provide uninformed feedback. (Use Documentation to fix this).
  - Tell them only what they need to know, and they will stay hyper-focused, but ultimately unengaged.

DIFFICULTY

I will only cover this briefly as the difficulty spectrum is beyond the scope of this book. Games are intended to be fun *and* challenging. Be mindful of your game's difficulty and test constantly with devs and non-devs, especially those in the target demographic.

'Let the Wookie win.'

Games are escapism. If the game is too hard it becomes a chore and players will shelve it. Let's continue.

COMMANDMENT 7: STORY

Story is one of the biggest retainers. Having a good story keeps people involved. If Game of Thrones was all fighting it wouldn't have lasted.

Story is where you craft;

- Who, What, When, Where, Why.
- Setting, Characters, Objectives, Mission, Awards.
- State Long Term Goal (LTG).
- Mid-Term Goal (MTG).
- Short Term Goal (STG).
- Visually communicate through:
    - Lighting
    - Layout
    - Landmark

EXAMPLE:

'To save the princess, we must defeat Bowser.' **-LTG**
'Get to the other castle' **-MTG**
'Get passed Goomba' **-STG**

WHO - CHARACTERS

Having interesting characters is key. Defining who they are will drive dialogue and motivations. Each character should have two to three traits and a quirk of some kind. These four-corners will define the box that defines the character. For the character to grow, they will need to venture outside of their box. The box also defines how they interact with other characters.

A great way to practice character development it to lay down, close your eyes, and imagine you are the character. Have a conversation with someone you know, or another character. You will have instant in-game and flowing dialogue. Write it down, then do it again. Change words that are clunky and bring out the traits in each character.

WHAT - WHERE - WHEN - SETTING GOALS

We can show a player a single image of a game world and they should have a good feel for what the game is about, where it is and what is happening. You will want to continually reiterate LTG, MTG, and STG through layout, VO and gameplay.

WHY - AWARD

To rescue the princess. Risk-reward is a big motivator. If the payoff is small, the player is less likely to engage. If the payoff is huge - the players will engage. If payoff is too big, it will lose value and the game will become imbalanced. What happens if the player character starts your game with the ultimate weapon?

Level layout will play a key part in defining and structuring the goals of the game. In Half-Life, the black tower is almost always visible in the distance. When Freeman eventually arrives, it is a massive payoff.

'Holy shit. I made it.' -Everyone.

The long term goal is realized.

Commandment 6 covered Iteration - the same holds true for Story. To craft a story, start with an eight-part outline exactly the same as a movie script, then iterate.

- Sequence 1 - Establish 'What' Problem 1 - **LTG**
- Sequence 2 - Details - **STG**
- Sequence 3 - Major Problem 2 - **MTG**
- Sequence 4 - Midpoint - **STG**
- Sequence 5 - Subplot - **STG**
- Sequence 6 - Wrap up Problem 2 - **MTG**
- Sequence 7 - Wrap up Subplot - **STG**
- Sequence 8 - Climax - Wrap up Problem 1 - **LTG**

Setting up a story this way gives it flow. The middle sequences are all fluid and can be moved around. We establish the long-term goal and bounce back and forth between short and mid-term goals until all obstacles are bypassed or resolved and the long-term goal completed. In movies, sequences are set by different types of shots, and the action, drama and dialogue are cut to match.

<u>Example:</u>

    Establishing Shot - Diner Exterior
    Medium Shot - Diner Interior
    Medium Shot - Table with Couple
    Close Up - Man
    Close Up - Woman
    Close Up - Man
    Close Up - Woman
    Medium Shot - Table with Couple
    Medium Shot - Diner Interior
    Establishing Shot - Diner Exterior

The scene has flow. A game is no different. Establish where you are and what you are doing and refer back to each frequently. Enemies or puzzles are good short-term goals. A level, or chapter is a good mid-term goal. Rescuing the princess is the long-term goal.

A game can tell a story without a single word of dialogue or written text. There are three keys to good level design that can tell the story on a subconscious level without ever speaking a single word of dialogue.

3 Keys: The Three 'L's'
- LIGHTING
- LAYOUT
- LANDMARK

These three keys are vital to design and development. This is good practice and also good for games on a tight budget - VO adds up quick.

LIGHTING

Lighting can tell a story entirely on its own - black and white. No color, only silhouette and shape. Chiaroscuro. Line drawings and sketches in black and white tell you everything you need to know. Storyboards and sketches - a picture is created before anything is built. Players can be drawn to lights, colors and contrast. If you stick a player in a dark room with a single light on the other side, you know damn well where they are going. Also, stick a pick-up on the other side to reward the exploration. A good artist will paint with light. Lighting and contrast can move players through an area.

LAYOUT

Layout is critical to game flow. Is your game linear or a loop? Does the area make sense? Can it be built with modules? What unique assets will you need?

In Fallout New Vegas, House's Lucky 38 secret room was originally a small, closet-like side room. An afterthought. It didn't say 'I run this town'. I created the 'Emperor's Chamber' - the hidden control room from which House controlled Vegas. The Throne Room. House was the heart and mind of the Lucky 38. If House had been shoved in a closet it would have changed his identity and power entirely.

On Deadpool, the area layouts matched the original concept art - mutant skyscrapers, mutant utopia, a wondrous open-world mutant-centric plaza. The initial internal videos were awesome and got the team on-board. After a beleaguered and a slashed development process we were told to wrap it up ASAP. When the levels were handed off to art, rooms were filled with filing cabinets and cubicle walls. Why would mutants need an island full of filing cabinets and cubicles? Who works here? It made no sense. It was a minor issue that nobody questioned - but still - stay diligent in keeping with the theme when laying out the levels. The more depth the layout has, the better the subconscious communication. If it doesn't make sense, the subconscious mind will pick up on it and label it as average or uninspired and they will shelve your game.

- Layout identifies and supports **LTG**, **MTG** and **STG**.

Both voiceover (VO) and layout work in tandem to identify, reiterate and reinforce goals. VO is not necessary, but it doesn't hurt. Many, many games rely heavily on companions or guides to help remind the player of their goals. VO is expensive and time consuming. You will want a writer and a script producer who focuses entirely on recording and implementing lines in tandem with your designers. As script edits occur, the lines will need to be re-recorded, if already recorded, then re-implemented in-game. Be mindful if this is necessary and within budget and timeframe. It adds up quickly - text only and sound effects are alternatives.

'Listen!'

Camera is also critical and many studios will have one or two devs assigned specifically to camera development. Camera is vital since it is the manner in which player's view the game world and layout. During testing, if you find that player's are getting lost, you must reassess layout and landmarks.

LANDMARKS

Landmarks are a way to communicate with the player and guide them to goals. If you have a (LTG) - Giant Floating Fortress in the distance, and (MTG) large dome-shaped building in the mid-ground, and a (STG) tiled road in the foreground, chances are players will subconsciously understand where they need to go.

'To get to the tower, I go to the dome and follow the road.'

If the player loses sight of the LTG, or if the LTG is not clearly identified they will feel that they are not progressing and shelve your game.

If players become lost in a maze of samey layout, they will become frustrated and shelve your game.

On Legacy of Kain: Defiance, we had a section of the game where Raziel had to go underwater and cut through a wall of rocks. Players internally were getting stuck and didn't know where to go. Producers came to my cube-mate and pal, Darren and asked if he could cut up the rocks to make them look more breakable or more readable as a breakable. We hadn't identified or trained players that these types of walls were breakable up to this point - which was a much larger design and development issue overall. I suggested we add a simple bubbles particle effect to the wall cracks which instantly communicated that it was breakable. A super-simple solution and players were no longer getting stuck. This was a band-aid solution however - and we needed to identify how we were teaching players the rules of the game.

- Rules must be taught and reinforced.

Landmarks are vital to level flow - during initial level creation (called blockout at many studios), drop in large unique placeholder meshes to identify where they are and how they can be seen. If the player can't see these meshes, they will literally lose sight of goals and get lost.

Let's continue.

COMMANDMENT 8: LOOP

There are two loops we will discuss;
- Business loop
- Gameplay loop

BUSINESS LOOP - PLAN FOR EXPANSION

Assume you will have success and design 5, 10, and 50 year plans. A couple of years ago I was heavily involved in some tech investor groups - their biggest piece of advice was *'write down the long term plan.'* I had aspirations for these massive IP's but no plan in place to actually develop them. I had a very detailed road map for a game, but no map for the ensuing DLC, sequel or other products I wanted to develop.

'Spaceballs the FLAMETHROWER!'

As soon as I started plugging in the different products, I realized there were gaping holes and major timeline issues. The LTG hadn't been established in my own business, so I had no roadmap to get to it.

Imagine Walt Disney's initial plan; 'make an animation.' Do you think he planned (they) would be buying the Star Wars license a generation later? No way. It wasn't even conceived yet - but setting the proper foundation gave Disney the capital to make the purchase - make new movies and bathe in a money bin. Disney has a long-term plan, acquires new IP or generates their own based on trends. Disney is a lifestyle, like Apple or Harley Davidson.

Your corporate loop must look to the future and have the same LTG, MTG and STG as a game.

GAMEPLAY LOOP

The game itself must have a tight and consistent game loop in order to keep player's interested.

- Much like the core mechanic - you must develop your tight game loop.
- This also has implications for the long-term loop:
    - How do you expand on your core mechanic and game world?
    - If you rescue the princess, what happens next game?
        - Mario cannot kill Bowser.
        - Batman cannot kill Joker.

Imagine if Batman packs a revolver and just straight-up *offs* the Joker with a dome shot.

- It would completely change his character.
- It would end the series.

Batman being noble, not using guns, and taking the moral high ground, gives the series an infinite loop.

- Batman can never win.

This theme does double duty as the brooding Bat's work is never done.

Example:

In Mario we:
- Jump over enemies.
- Touch the flag.

In Alpha Protocol, the game loop was;
- Safe House.
- Mission.
- Cinematic.

Think about your favorite game and back engineer the game loop. Write your own game loop. Iterate on the loop until it is watertight and fun. If your core mechanic, your hook and your loop are boring, too long or uninspired, they will shelve your game. Let's continue.

COMMANDMENT 9: DOCUMENTS

Documentation is one of the most maligned features of development. The majority of devs won't read it, but it must be written to give the team tasks, timeline and reference. If there is no documentation, the game will be a malleable ball of clay and never fit into the box, as it will continue to reshape and shift around undefined goals and design pillars. This is often referred to as feature creep.

DESIGN PILLARS
- Choose 2-3 keywords that the game is about.
- Write them down.
- Discuss.

On Tomb Raider, when Lead Designer Riley Cooper pitched the team on the pillars - there was no COMBAT pillar anywhere to be seen. The team was aghast. How can we have a TR game without combat? Simply put, we have combat and it will be good - but it isn't the focus. The focus was on Lara's movement, exploration and puzzles. It was an adventure game, not a shooter.

'Wouldn't it be cool if...'

FEATURE CREEP
As soon as you hear the words above, your alarm should go off. Write these ideas down - as they may be good, or spawn something innovative - but be ultra-ultra careful that you don't include them at the cost of the schedule. If you are adding something during development - be sure that it will fit. A simple feature added at any time has

long-term ramifications. Multiple features will surely sink your ship.

So, why document?

- As soon as you write it down it becomes real and you can act on it.
- Makes a list of things you want to make.
- You will immediately find that there are gaping holes in your idea.
- Fill those holes.
- Repeat.
- This becomes part of the iteration process.
- Devs can refer to it and become grounded, or
- Provide feedback!

Documentation is vital to hand off to anyone that comes aboard - they can read a doc and understand. You must be able to communicate effectively with your team. You can be sitting side-by-side with someone at the same screen and still miscommunicate. This is compounded when team members are remote.

- COMMUNICATION is the #1 issue for all companies.

GOOD DOCUMENTATION

Good documentation must be clear and concise. When writing a document do not exceed:

- 10 bullet points.
- One Line for each.

At Obsidian, I had just shipped Fallout and was moved to help ship Dungeon Siege. We were using a new proprietary engine. *(That would later be used on Pillars of Eternity, I believe.)* I was given new, unfinished tools to develop content. I asked for documentation, and there wasn't any. I asked where and what the story was about, and nobody knew. **This is completely common across all studios.** As part of familiarizing myself with the project, I began asking questions and documenting my findings. This took roughly four man-hours - My time and the time of the devs I was talking to. The documentation for DS was lengthy. When developing an RPG, especially one with depth, it needs massive amounts of documentation. However, there was no single story summary for what happens and why. The team wasn't on board because nobody knew what they were making or why. I read the 'story bible' and summarized key events and story branches in a 1-page document and sent it to the team.

- Write a 10-point document for your favorite game.
- Then write your own game doc. Do it now and come back to this book.

Tomb Raider's documentation was massive. If memory serves, it was several 4-inch binders detailing everything you ever wanted to know about Lara and the license. Only one designer ever read it. *He was also our best designer.* When working on an IP as huge and long-lasting as TR, the documentation will often cover what has happened in previous titles. Be mindful of length - but be sure to document it. Plan for future expansion. Let's continue.

COMMANDMENT 10: SHIP

A game that never ships is just a jumble of ideas and what-could-have-beens. You must ship your product and deliver on time. Keep in mind the following, and refer to them often;

- Target release date.
- Competition / Game trends.
- Console life.
- Bugs.

'Ship It!'

TARGET RELEASE DATE

When you first join a studio you will here this mantra often - and repeated a lot the closer to ship date. It helps the team stay focused on the Long Term Goal: Ship the game, earn the studio money. Make more games - *that are an improvement over what was made before.*

Everyone has a game idea - the ones that complete their product are the ones that generate revenue. Simple enough.

COMPETITION

When first documenting your game, think of what is out there and how to improve on it. What are the next logical evolutions of gameplay? Who is doing what we want to do? Technology evolves extremely quickly and you must stay on top of competition and trends.

CONSOLE LIFE

If you are targeting consoles, be mindful of their lifespan. You don't want to be developing for a console that will rotate at the end of it's lifecycle. Nobody wants old and busted.

BUGS

It has become an inside joke in the game and tech community that when something colossally fucked up occurs - someone will utter *'ship it'* - meaning - we can't ship with this in the game. Bug fixing occurs during and throughout the dev process. Young devs will often put off the debugging phase until the end of the cycle or milestone - this is a huge error for many reasons;

- Fixing a bug or addressing the issue will often uncover other issues.
- Fighting through the bug - will allow you to address entirely new ones.
- When the milestone hits - bug fixing is the name of the game for a good 1/3 of your timeline. That can be months on a larger project and large bug lists will bury you.

I've never shipped a bug-free game and the larger the title the higher volume of egregious bugs get waived - since pushing back will cost a studio (and publisher and console developer) hundreds of thousands if not millions of dollars - and the bug can always be patched in the 2-week down time from submission to approval to consumer.

- Give yourself roughly one-third to one-quarter of your total dev-time to bug fixing.
- Give yourself a month or three to submit, fix, and submit again to complete your project.

Shipping the game on time is critical. You must keep your eye on the prize and deliver. Let's continue.

COMMANDMENT 11: RULES

Fuck the Rules - you are in charge of your future, make tomorrow a new chapter. There are no set rules and everything is flexible. You decide what you will do.

Can you write down the 10 Commandments on the lines below? Make some cheat sheets to help you remember them and refer back to this book often.

Remember, reading a book about games and playing games doesn't make you a better game dev. Making games makes you a better game dev. Get started today, you will wish you started sooner. Let's get started.

ABOUT THE AUTHOR

J.R. Vosovic

J.R has been developing video games since 2000 and diversified into transmedia, tabletop games and VR in 2013. He triple-majored at Cal State University, Chico under the Computer Graphics Special Major. *10 Commandments* is the culmination of over 20 years of professional game development experience.

Thank you.